Girl Talk

Women on Life, Love,
and Getting What You Want

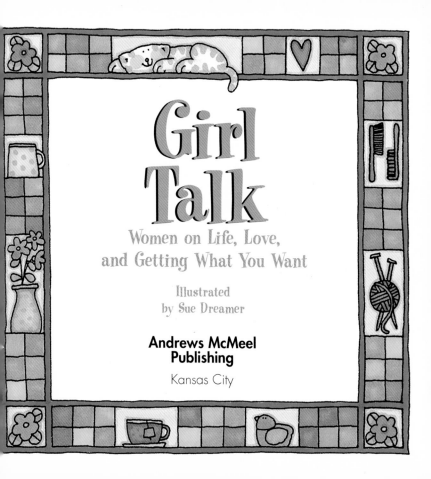

Girl Talk

Women on Life, Love, and Getting What You Want

Illustrated
by Sue Dreamer

Andrews McMeel
Publishing

Kansas City

Girl Talk is a property exclusively licensed through Applejack Licensing International of Manchester, Vermont 05255. For further information call (802) 362-3662.

Illustrations © Sue Dreamer 1999
Courtesy of Applejack Licensing International/Lionheart Books, Ltd.
Design & Compilation © 1999 Lionheart Books, Ltd.

Girl Talk was produced by Lionheart Books, Ltd.,
5105 Peachtree Industrial Boulevard, Atlanta, Georgia 30341

Design: Carley Wilson Brown

www.andrewsmcmeel.com

ISBN: 0-7407-0090-1

Library of Congress Catalog Card Number: 99-72682

Introduction

Girltalk—it's the language of women that covers everything from where to buy the best shoes to how to recover from a broken heart. It is something we rely on from childhood to old age to encourage us, keep us on track, to make us laugh when we need to, and cry if we want to. When women want an honest opinion, they usually go to their women friends—who else would we trust to tell us what we need to hear even when  we don't want to hear it? Our girlfriends are our most reliable confidantes, and their wonderful way of seeing to the heart of the matter is part of why we love and cherish them.

Whether it's helpful hints about love, children, work, marriage, or housekeeping, women are never at a loss for words. Words that unravel life's tangles with candor, humor, affection and, best of all, experience. This selection of quotes from women for women ranges from witty, funny observations to inspiring, thoughtful commentaries, but there's one thing they all share: common sense.

Advice like "you just have to learn not to care about the dust-mice under the beds," or "the mere sense of living is joy enough" reminds us of the magical way our girlfriends, old and new, have of putting things into perspective. Here is a book that celebrates those essential ties and the way they enrich our lives, our loves, and our dreams.

Continuity gives us roots; change gives us branches,

letting us stretch and grow and reach new heights.

Pauline R. Kezer

When women get depressed
they either eat or go shopping.
Men invade another country.

Elayne Boosler

never bend your head.

hold it high.

look the world straight in the eye.

Helen Keller

Luck is a matter of preparation
meeting opportunity.

Oprah Winfrey

You just have to learn not to care about
the dust-mice under the beds.

Margaret Mead

There is time
for work. And
time for love.
That leaves
no other
time.

Coco Chanel

I've always been independent, and I don't s

w it conflicts with my femininity. Sylvia Porter

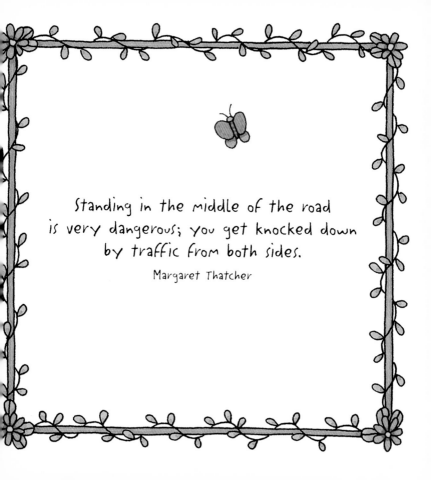

Standing in the middle of the road
is very dangerous; you get knocked down
by traffic from both sides.

Margaret Thatcher

The mere sense of living is joy enough.
Emily Dickinson

The way I see it, if you want the rainbow, you gotta put up with the rain.

Dolly Parton

Florence Kennedy

You cannot always have happiness, but you can always give happiness.
Anonymous

To be kind to all, to like many and love a few, to be needed and wanted by those we love, is certainly the nearest we can come to happiness.

Mary Roberts Rinehart

Work is either fun or
drudgery. It depends on
your attitude. I like fun.

Colleen C. Barrett

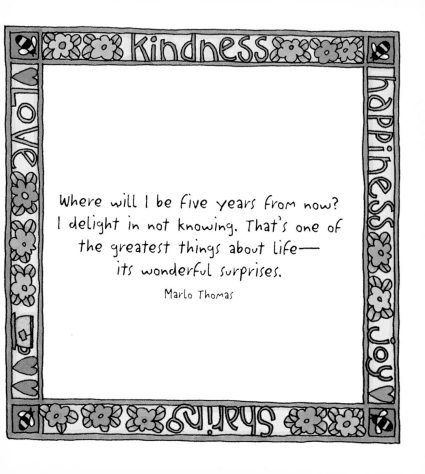

Where will I be five years from now?
I delight in not knowing. That's one of
the greatest things about life—
its wonderful surprises.

Marlo Thomas

It matters more what's in a woman's face
than what's on it.

Claudette Colbert

Sexiness wears thin after a while and beauty
fades, but to be married to a man who makes you
laugh every day, ah, now that's a real treat.

Joanne Woodward

Instant gratification takes too long.

Carrie Fisher

Sow good services; sweet remembrances
will grow from them.

Mme. de Stael

The most called-upon prerequisite of a friend is an accessible ear.

Maya Angelou

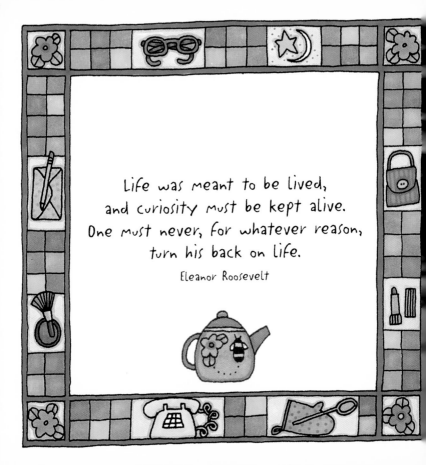

Life was meant to be lived,
and curiosity must be kept alive.
One must never, for whatever reason,
turn his back on life.

Eleanor Roosevelt

To love what you do and feel that it matters—how could anything be more fun!

Katherine Graham

Good friends

Smiles

Secrets

Good books

A happy woman
is one who has no cares at all;
a cheerful woman is one who has cares
but doesn't let them get her down.

Beverly Sills

Laugh ☆ dream

An aim in life is the only fortune worth finding.

Jacqueline Kennedy Onassis

Cleaning your house while your kids are still growi

like shoveling the walk before it stops snowing.

Phyllis Diller

Never eat more than you can lift.

Miss Piggy

friends and flowers are charming while they are fresh.

Mme. de Sartory

Age doesn't protect you from love.
But love, to some extent,
protects you from age.

Jeanne Moreau

Snowflakes are one of nature's most fragile things,
but just look what they can do
when they stick together.

Vesta M. Kelly

Life begets life. Energy creates energy.

It is by spending oneself that one becomes rich.

Sarah Bernhardt

I never hated a man enough
to give him his diamonds back.

Zsa Zsa Gabor

Flops are parts of life's menu,
and I've never been a girl to miss out
on any of the courses.

Rosalind Russell

The quickest way to know a woman
is to go shopping with her.

Marcelene Cox

One must never look for happiness: One meets

the way. Isabelle Eberhardt

Happiness is not perfected until it is shared.

Jayne Porter

I've always believed that one woman's success

can only help another woman's success.

Gloria Vanderbilt

It is easy to be independent when you've got money.
But to be independent when you haven't got
a thing—that's the Lord's test.

Mahalia Jackson

People are like stained-glass windows.
They sparkle and shine when the sun is out, but when
the darkness sets in, their true beauty is revealed
only if there is a light from within.

Elizabeth Kubler-Ross

Fear less, hope more; eat less, chew more;
whine less, breathe more; talk less,
say more; love more, and all good things
will be yours.

Swedish proverb

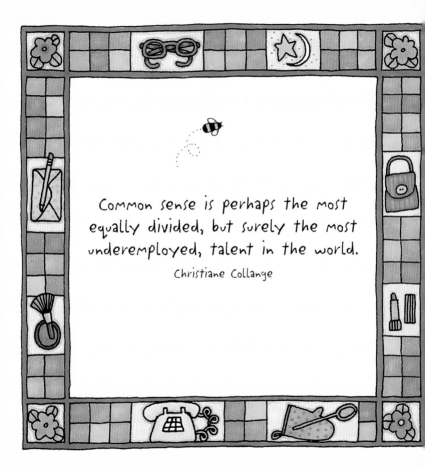

Common sense is perhaps the most equally divided, but surely the most underemployed, talent in the world.

Christiane Collange

God gives every bird his worm, but He does not throw it into the nest.

P. D. James

I look back on my life like a good day's work;
it is done and I am satisfied with it.

Grandma Moses

To have ideas is to gather flowers;
to think is to weave them into garlands.

Anne Sophie Swetchine

Far away in the sunshine are my highest aspirations. I may not reach them, but I can look up and see the beauty, believe in them, and try to follow where they lead.

Louisa May Alcott

I was not looking for my
dreams to interpret my life,
but rather for my life to
interpret my dreams.

Susan Sontag

Scatter seeds of kindness everywhere you go;

Scatter bits of courtesy—watch them grow and grow.

Gather buds of friendship; keep them till full-blown;

You will find more happiness than you have ever known.
Amy R. Raabe

If you want a thing well done, get a couple of old broads to do it.

Bette Davis